978   c.2

VISSCHER.
    THE PONY EXPRESS.

1980   3.95   3-90

THE NEWS OF LINCOLN'S ELECTION

"Away across the endless dead level of the prairie a black speck appears. In a second or two it becomes a horse and rider . . . sweeping toward us . . . another instant a whoop and a hurrah from our upper deck, a wave of the rider's hand . . . and man and horse burst past our excited faces, and go winging away like a belated fragment of a storm."

Mark Twain, in *Roughing It*

THE PONY EXPRESS

A THRILLING AND TRUTHFUL HISTORY

AND OTHER SKETCHES AND INCIDENTS OF THOSE STIRRING TIMES

by

WILLIAM LIGHTFOOT VISSCHER
1908

C. 2

978
VISSCHER

This booklet is excerpted from
the antique original book, with illustrations
from that source and others
added from *The Great Salt Lake Trail*
(1898), *Century* (1888, 1889, 1898),
Crofutt's Overland Tours (1888),
Colorado – its gold and silver mines (1880), Scribner's Magazine (1889 and 1895),
and *Harper's Weekly* (1867). Wells Fargo and Bancroft Library helped with illustrations, too. Gary Hurelle drew the map in the center.

ISBN 0-89646-062-2

CONTENTS

PURSUIT OF EXPRESS MAIL-CARRIER.

In the Rocky Mountains

Rand McNally Co.

THE GOLD FEVER

THE discovery of gold in California, in the richest and most accessible deposits ever known in the world, of which there is authentic account, had sent a mighty stream of humanity to that region. Its currents had arisen throughout the earth, and converging there, had flooded the region.

"The fall of '49 and spring of '50" were the times of the greatest tides savages killed thousands. The trail was marked with skeletons and scattered bones of human beings and animals of all kinds. The history of it all groans with pain, privation, and death. The details of adventure that have been written and printed would load a long railway train, and yet the half has not been told.

Notwithstanding the struggle necessary to get there, people in long and

"THE CENTRAL ROUTE"

of immigration. By sail from the uttermost parts of the earth people had gone along all the ways necessary to reach the land of gold and from the relatively eastern regions of this republic, men, women, and children had taken the "Isthmus Route" and "Round the Horn," long voyages by sea, for the same goal. Countless thousands had also toiled across the plains and mountains, "The Overland Route." To use the mildest terms, it was a strenuous journey. Disease, fatigue, flood, cold, heat, storms, and lustful lines arrived and immediately sought "the diggings," or fell into other ways of attaining the yellow bait. Commerce in all branches of trade, gambling, robbery, anything to get gold was done. Not all men in all these ways struggled for it, but some men in each. At any rate the magnet drew people in such numbers that California quickly received inhabitants enough to be admitted to the Union as a State, and as the territory belonged to this republic, one of the United States.

Government was rapidly systema-
tized, and business with "the States,"
was needful, mandatory, strong, and
intense. The distance and the perilous and time-consuming means of
communication made an ever-pend-
ing obstacle to all the ramifications
of life between the new state and the
older states, commercial, govern-
mental, social. Leading men were
constantly calculating ways and
means and endeavoring to evolve plans
for the bettering of these conditions.

Hon. W. M. Gwin, one of the United
States Senators from California, pro-
ceeding in the fall of 1854 from San
Francisco to Washington City, to
take up his legislative duties, rode,
horseback, from the Pacific Ocean to
the Missouri River, by the way of
Sacramento, Salt Lake City, South
Pass, and down the Platte to St.
Joseph, that way then known as
"The Central Route."

One of the standing jokes of that
day was that the term of a member
of Congress from California might
run out while he was on the way to
the national capital, if he was much
delayed, en route.

On a long distance of the journey
mentioned, and for many days, Senator Gwin had for a traveling companion Mr. B. F. Ficklin, general
superintendent of the pioneer freighting firm, Russell, Majors and Waddell. Between these two earnest,
observant, and practical men grew
the idea, on this journey, of what
afterward culminated in the famous
"Pony Express." Both were enthusiastic for closer communication between California and the East, and
the Senator became an active and
untiring advocate of the freighter's
scheme for the unique express service
mentioned.

In January following (1855), and

Senator
Gwinn

almost immediately after Senator
Gwin's arrival in Washington, he
introduced a bill in Congress looking
to the establishment of a weekly mail
express between St. Louis and San
Francisco. The time schedule of
this service was to be ten days
between the two cities. Five thousand dollars for the round trip was to
be the compensation and the Central
Route to be the line traveled.

That bill went to the Senate Com-
mittee on Military Affairs, and it was
relegated to the reserves. At any
rate its front never showed again.

"The Irrepressible Conflict" was
on for the following five years, until
the election of Mr. Lincoln as president precipitated the Civil War, and
during all this time Congress and the
country east were so entirely ab-
sorbed in the impending struggle that
nearly all thought of Pacific Coast
business was submerged in the inten-
sity of sectional affairs. But the far
West, especially California, clamored
more and louder for accelerated mail
service. The people of these regions
desired to know what was going on

and were insistent. The war talk was added to all the other causes of the demand for quicker information. Thus, the West did not cease to agitate the subject.

The South, however, was strongest in Congress. Its interests, pending the struggle, demanded the prevention of legislation favorable to the routes north of "Mason and Dixon's Line" and sought the confining of all government aid in that direction to the southern routes.

In those days there were three trans-continental mail routes, very slow ones, but the great bulk of the mail was sent by the Isthmian Route, via Panama, and the time between New York and San Francisco, at its best, was twenty-two days.

The first overland mail route west of the Missouri was a monthly stage line from Independence to Salt Lake, 1,200 miles. Its first trip began July 1, 1850, and its continuance was four years. In 1854, the Government paid $80,000 per annum for a monthly mail-stage from Missouri, via Albuquerque, to Stockton, California. It was one of the failures of the period—during the nine months it ran, its receipts were $1,255. Thus early, as well as later, there were many serious interruptions in the service. The eastern mails for November, 1850, reached California in March, 1851; and the news of the creation of Utah Territory by Congress in September, 1850, arrived at Salt Lake the following January, having gone via Panama by steamer to San Francisco, and thence east by private messenger.

STANDING OFF INDIANS.

Newspaper cut of a Pony Express
Rider published in 1860

THE MOST UNIQUE AND ROMANTIC
MAIL SERVICE EVER ORGANIZED

DESPITE the consuming interest in the coming war, Senator Gwin kept up his fight for a quick mail route and the reduction of time in sending news to the Pacific Coast and receiving news from that region. Notwithstanding that it was found impossible to obtain any subsidy from Congress, at that time, for the purpose in view, in the winter of 1859–60, Senator Gwin and several capitalists of New York, and Mr. Russell of the Overland transportation firm of Russell, Majors and Waddell, met in Washington City, and the result of that meeting was the real start of one of the most romantic and daring business ventures this country, or any other country, ever knew. That was the Pony Express. By that the time of transmitting news across the continent was reduced from twenty-one days to ten days. It is about 3,500 miles by our most direct railway route from New York to San Francisco, and it took seven days, three hours, and forty-five minutes actual time to cover the distance on our fastest express trains during the first years of railroad history. In 1859, there was not a mile of railroad west of the Missouri River. St. Joseph, Missouri, was the western terminus of railway communication, and between that city and the young city of the Golden Gate there intervened but one city, Salt Lake, and 2,000 miles of wild, uninhabited country, infested with warlike Indians. Through this uninviting region led the trails over which it was proposed to ride the flying ponies.

Genghis Khan, the remarkable conqueror of Tartary and China, who flourished in the years between A. D. 1203 and 1227, has lately received the credit of having originated the Pony Express. Some one has looked up the fact in the writings of Marco Polo, who says that the ancient Tartar had stations every twenty-five miles over the territory that he wished to send messages, and that his riders made nothing of covering 300 miles a day. However, things have ample time to grow in some centuries, and these rides may have been stretched considerably on the elastic paper used in Polo's time. It is certain, though, that the system has been used in Asia and Europe, even within a century, and may be used there yet in remote regions. It is also certain that pony express was used in this country about the middle of the first half of the last century. That is to say, two or three decades before the Pony Express across the Great American Desert. David Hale, an enterprising New York newspaper man, used it about 1825 in collecting state news. In 1830, Richard Haughton, editor of the New York Journal of Commerce, afterward founder of the Boston Atlas, utilized the system in the collection of election returns. James Watson Webb, of the New York Courier and Enquirer, established a pony express in 1832 between New York and Washington that wrought dismay among his competitors until railways and telegraphs overlapped him.

These enterprises were, however, as simple and harmless as roller skating compared to the dangers and tests of endurance to which the Pony Express riders of the western plains and mountains were subjected in 1860–61.

Majors, Russell and Waddell established and maintained for a number of years a fourteen-day mail schedule by rail and pony express between New York and San Francisco, making the trip of the running ponies from St. Joseph to Sacramento as exactly upon the schedule time as do our mails to-day. By using the telegraph to St. Joe and the pony express beyond, news was carried from ocean to ocean in ten days.

Senator Gwin's strongest argument was that if the operating company could carry the mails to the Pacific Coast in quicker time than was then being accomplished, and if it could be shown that the line might be kept open the year round, increased emigration and the building of a railroad by the Government would result. The sequel has far exceeded the most extravagant hopes of all who were then concerned.

This able and patriotic statesman who had so deeply interested himself in the project under consideration, not only for the reasons already given, but also in the interest of accelerating communication between the Unionists of the Pacific Coast and the Federal authorities, ended strangely. Stalwart Union senator that he was, he afterward espoused the cause of the Southern Confederacy, when his native state, Mississippi, seceded, and by so doing lost his great prestige, influence, and fortune in California. After the war he drifted into Mexico

and the service of the ill-starred Emperor Maximilian, who, in 1866, made him Duke of Sonora in the furtherance of the visionary scheme of western empire. But Gwin shortly afterward died.

Col. Alexander Majors, who long survived his partners, and wrote a highly interesting and instructive book of strictest authenticity, entitled "Seventy Years on the Frontier," gives in substance the following history of the Pony Express, which account necessarily repeats in a few brief instances some of the preceding matter in this chronicle.

Col. Majors says that in the winter of 1859, while the senior member of the firm was in Washington, he became intimately acquainted with Senator Gwin, of California, who, as stated previously, was very anxious that a quicker line for the transmission of letters should be established than that already worked by Butterfield; the latter was outrageously circuitous.

The senator was acquainted with the fact that the firm of Russell, Majors, and Waddell were operating a daily coach from the Missouri River to Salt Lake City, and he urged Mr. Russell to consider seriously the propriety of starting a pony express over the same route, and from Salt Lake City on to Sacramento.

After a lengthy consultation with Senator Gwin, Mr. Russell consented to attempt the thing, provided he could induce his partners to take the same view of the proposed enterprise as himself, and he then returned to Leavenworth, the headquarters of the firm, to consult the other members. On learning the proposition suggested by Senator Gwin, both Colonel Majors and Mr. Waddell at once decided that the expense would be much greater than any possible revenue from the undertaking.

FREDERIC REMINGTON.

CHANGING HORSES.

Mr. Russell, having, as he thought, partly at least, committed himself to the Senator, was much chagrined at the turn the affair had taken, and he declared that he could not abandon his promise to Mr. Gwin, consequently his partners must stand by him.

That urgent appeal settled the question, and work was commenced to start the Pony Express.

On the Overland Stage Line, operated by the firm, stations had been located every ten or twelve miles, which were at once utilized for the operation of the express; but beyond Salt Lake City new stations must be constructed, as there were no possible stopping places on the proposed new route. In less than two months after the promise of the firm had been pledged to Senator Gwin, the first express was ready to leave San Francisco and St. Joseph, Missouri, simultaneously.

The fastest time ever thus far made on the "Butterfield Route" was twenty-one days between San Francisco and New York. The Pony Express curtailed that time at once by eleven days, which was a marvel of rapid transit at that period.

The plant necessary to meet the heavy demand made on the originators of the fast mail route over the barren plains and through the dangerous mountains was nearly five hundred horses, one hundred and ninety stations, and eighty experienced riders, each of whom was to make an average of thirty-three and one-third miles. To accomplish this, each man used three ponies on his route, but in cases of great emergency much longer distances were made.

As suggested by two members of the firm, when they protested that the business would not begin to meet the expenses, their prophecies proved true; but they were not disappointed, for one of the main objects of the institution of the express was to learn whether the line through which the express was carried could be made a permanent one for travel during all the seasons of the year. This was determined in the affirmative.

In the spring of 1860, Bolivar

DRAWN BY FERNAND LUNGREN.

WAITING ON THE TRAIL WITH A RELAY PONY.

Roberts, superintendent of the western division of the Pony Express, went to Carson City, Nevada, to engage riders and station agents for the Pony Express route across the Great Plains. In a few days fifty or sixty riders were engaged—men noted for their lithe, wiry physiques, bravery and coolness in moments of great personal danger, and endurance under the most trying circumstances of fatigue. Particularly were these requirements necessary in those who were to ride over the lonely route. It was no easy duty; horse and human flesh were strained to the limit of physical tension. Day or night, in sunshine or in storm, under the darkest skies, in the pale moonlight, and with only the stars at times to guide him, the brave rider must speed on. Rain, hail, snow, or sleet, there was no delay; his precious burden of letters demanded his best efforts under the stern necessities of the hazardous service; it brooked no detention; on he must ride. Sometimes his pathway led across level prairies, straight as the flight of an arrow. It was oftener a zigzag trail hugging the brink of awful precipices and dark, narrow cañons infested with watchful savages, eager for the scalp of the daring man who had the temerity to enter their mountain fastnesses.

At the stations the rider must be ever ready for emergencies; fre-

quently double duty was assigned him. Perhaps he whom he was to relieve had been murdered by the Indians, or so badly wounded that it was impossible for him to take his tour; then the already tired express-man must take his place and be off like a shot, although he had been in the saddle for hours.

The ponies employed in the service were splendid specimens of speed and endurance; they were fed and housed with the greatest care, for their mettle must never fail the test to which it was put. Ten miles distance at the limit of the animal's pace was exacted from him, and he came dashing into the station flecked with foam, nostrils dilated, and every hair reeking with perspiration, while his flanks thumped at every breath.

Nearly two thousand miles in eight days must be made; there was no idling for man or beast. When the express rode up to the station, both rider and pony were always ready. The only delay was a second or two as the saddle pouch with its precious burden was thrown on and the rider leaped into his place, then away they rushed down the trail, and in a moment were out of sight.

Two hundred and fifty miles a day was the distance traveled by the Pony Express, and it may be assured the rider carried no surplus weight. Neither he nor his pony were handicapped with anything that was not absolutely necessary. Even his case of precious letters made a bundle no larger than an ordinary writing tablet, but there was $5.00 paid in advance for every letter transported across the continent. Their bulk was not in the least commensurable with their number; there were hundreds of them sometimes, for they were written on the thinnest tissue

paper to be procured. There were no silly love missives among them nor frivolous correspondence of any kind; business letters only that demanded the most rapid transit possible and warranted the immense expense attending their journey found their way by the Pony Express.

The mail-bags were two pouches of leather, impervious to rain, sealed, and strapped to the rider's saddle before and behind. The pouches were never to contain over twenty pounds in weight. Inside the pouches, to further protect their contents from the weather, the letters and despatches were wrapped in oil silk, then sealed. The pockets themselves were locked, and were not opened between St. Joseph and Sacramento.

The Pony Express, as a means of communication between the two remote coasts, was largely employed by the Government, merchants, and traders, and would eventually have been a paying venture had not the construction of the telegraph across the continent usurped its usefulness.

The arms of the Pony Express rider, in order to keep the weight at a minimum, were, as a rule, limited to revolver and knife.

The first trip from St. Joseph to San Francisco, 1966 in exact miles, was made in ten days; the second, in fourteen; the third, and many succeeding trips, in nine. The riders had a division of from one hundred to one hundred forty miles, with relays of horses at distances varying from twenty to twenty-five miles.

In 1860, the Pony Express made one trip from St. Joseph to Denver, 625 miles, in two days and twenty-one hours.

The Pony Express riders received from $120 to $125 a month. But few men can appreciate the danger and excitement to which those daring and plucky men were subjected; it can never be told in all its constant variety. They were men remarkable for their lightness of weight and energy. Their duty demanded the most consummate vigilance and agility. Many among their number were skillful guides, scouts, and couriers, and had passed eventful lives on the Great Plains and in the Rocky Mountains. They possessed strong wills and a determination that nothing in the ordinary course could balk. Their horses were generally half-breed California mustangs, as quick and full of endurance as their riders, and were as sure footed and fleet as a mountain goat; the facility and pace at which they traveled was a marvel. The Pony Express stations were scattered over a wild, desolate stretch of country, 2,000 miles long. The trail was infested with "road agents" and hostile savages who roamed in formidable bands, ready to murder and scalp with as little compunction as they would kill a buffalo.

Some portions of the dangerous route had to be covered at the astounding pace of twenty-five miles an hour, as the distance between stations was determined by the physical character of the region.

For the most part, the employes of the Pony Express were different from the plainsmen of the time, generally. The latter were usually boisterous, profane and intemperate. The organizers of the Pony Express were abstemious, moral and truthful men, and they sought to have their employes observe a high standard of integrity.

When the plans for the Pony Express had been sufficiently matured and all was in readiness to start on the day set, the enterprising firm that had organized the enterprise, and which owned it entirely and without Government subsidy, or other, that is to say

THE PONY EXPRESS.

the firm of Russell, Majors & Waddell, through Mr. Russell, who was the most enthusiastic and insistent, at first, of the members, caused the following advertisement to be published in the "New York Herald" of March 26, 1860, and the "Missouri Republican" of St. Louis, on the same date:

TO SAN FRANCISCO
IN EIGHT DAYS
—)BY(—
THE CENTRAL OVERLAND CALIFORNIA
—)AND(—
PIKE'S PEAK EXPRESS.

The first courier of the Pony Express will leave the Missouri River on Tuesday, April 3d, at 5 o'clock p. m., and will run regularly weekly thereafter, carrying a letter mail only. The point of departure on the Missouri River will be in telegraphic communication with the East and will be announced in due time.

Telegraphic messages from all parts of the United States and Canada, in connection with the point of departure will be received up to 5 o'clock p. m. of the day of leaving, and transmitted over the Placerville and St. Joseph telegraph wire to San Francisco and intermediate points, by the connecting express in eight days.

The letter mail will be delivered in San Francisco in ten days from the departure of the Express. The express passes through Forts Kearney, Laramie, and Bridger, Great Salt Lake City, Camp Floyd, Carson City, the Washoe Silver Mines, Placerville, and Sacramento.

Letters for Oregon, Washington Territory, British Columbia, the Pacific Mexican ports, Russian possessions, Sandwich Islands, China, Japan, and India will be mailed in San Francisco.

Special messengers, bearers of letters to connect with the express of the 3d of April, will receive communications for the courier of that day at No. 481 Tenth Street, Washington City, up to 2.45 p. m. on Friday, March 30, and in New York, at the office of J. B. Simpson, Room No. 8, Continental Bank Building, Nassau Street, up to 6.30 a. m. of March 31st.

Full particulars can be obtained on application at the above place and agents of the Company.

W. H. RUSSELL, President.
Leavenworth City, Kansas, March, 1860.
Office in New York, J. B. Simpson, Vice-President.

Samuel & Allen, Agents, St. Louis.
H. J. Spaulding, Agent, Chicago.

The Civil War began in nine months after the Pony Express was started, and never has news been more anxiously awaited than on the Pacific Coast during the existence of this enterprise. The first tidings of the attack on Fort Sumter was sent by the Pony Express, and its connections, to San Francisco in eight days, fourteen hours. From that time on a bonus was given by California business men and public officials to the Pony Express Company to be distributed among the riders for carrying war news as fast as possible. For bringing the news of the battle of Antietam to Sacramento one day earlier than usual, in 1861, a purse of $300 extra was collected for the riders.

During the last few weeks preceding the termination of the Pony Express, by the opening of the transcontinental telegraph, the express riders brought an average of 700 letters per week from the Pacific coast. In those last few weeks, after the telegraph had been completed to Fort Kearney, the "pony" rates were reduced to $1.00 per half ounce, and each letter was enclosed in a 10-cent Government stamped envelope for each half ounce, and this was the only financial interest the Government had, at any time, in the Pony Express enterprise, until the remnant of it was transferred by Russell, Majors & Waddell to the Wells-Fargo Company.

In all the trips across the continent, and the 650,000 miles ridden by the Pony Express riders of the Russell, Majors & Waddell Company, the record is that only one mail was lost, and that a comparatively small and unimportant one.

Notwithstanding that the packages of letters were wrapped in oil silk, they were sometimes injured by water when, occasionally, a rider was forced to swim his horse across a swollen stream. Once under such circumstances the horse was drowned, but the rider, with his mail, escaped.

When, on one occasion, the rider was killed by Indians, the pony escaped with the letter pouch which was subsequently recovered, and the letters were promptly forwarded to their destination.

Alexander Majors.

OFF BOTH WAYS

THE day of the first start, on the 3d of April, 1860, at noon, says Colonel Majors, Harry Roff, mounted on a spirited half-breed broncho, left Sacramento on his perilous ride, covering the first twenty miles, including one change, in fifty-nine minutes. On reaching Folsom he changed again and started for Placerville at the foot of the Sierra Nevada Mountains, fifty-five miles distant. There he connected with "Boston," who took the route to Friday's Station, crossing the eastern summit of the Sierra Nevada. Sam Hamilton next fell into line and pursued his way to Genoa, Carson City, Dayton, Reed's Station, and Fort Churchill, seventy-five miles. The entire run was made in fifteen hours and twenty-minutes, the entire distance being 185 miles, which included the crossing of the western summit of the Sierra Nevada through thirty feet of snow! Here Robert Haslam took the trail from Fort Churchill to Smith's Creek, 120 miles through a hostile Indian country. From that point Jay G. Kelley rode from Smith's Creek to Ruby Valley, Utah, 116 miles. From Ruby Valley to Deep Creek, H. Richardson, 105 miles. From Deep Creek to Rush Valley, old Camp Floyd, 80 miles; from Camp Floyd to Salt Lake City,

JAMES BUCHANAN
President of the United
States in those days

50 miles, the end of the western division—in all 130 miles—was ridden by George Thacher.

On the same day, and the same moment, Mr. Russell superintended the start of the Pony Express from its eastern terminus. An arrangement had been made with the railroads between New York and St. Joseph for a fast train which was scheduled to arrive with the mail at the proper time. The Hannibal & St. Joseph Railroad also ran a special engine, and the boat which made the crossing of the Missouri River was detained for the purpose of instantly transferring the letters. Mr. Russell in person adjusted the letter pouch on the pony. Many of the enthusiastic crowd, who had congregated to witness the inauguration of the fast mail, plucked hairs from the hardy little animal's tail as talismans of good luck. In a few seconds the rider was mounted, the steamboat gave an encouraging whistle, and the pony dashed away on his long journey to the next station.

There has been much discussion among those interested as to who rode the first horse out of St. Joseph at the opening of the Pony Express service, many claiming that the rider was John Frey. Mr. Huston Wyeth, a native of St. Joseph, and one of the most distinguished citizens of Missouri, wrote to his friend, J. H. Keetley, one of the first of the Pony Express riders, now at the head of an extensive mining concern at Salt Lake City, Utah, and Mr. Keetley replied in the following letter, a copy of which

Mr. Wyeth gave to the author of this book:

Salt Lake City, Utah, August 21, 1907

Mr. Huston Wyeth,

   St. Joseph, Mo.

Dear Sir:—

Yours of the 17th inst. received, and in reply will say that Alex Carlyle was the first man to ride the Pony Express out of St. Joe. He was a nephew of the superintendent of the stage line to Denver, called the "Pike's Peak Express." The superintendent's name was Ben Fickland. Carlyle was a consumptive, and could not stand the hardships, and retired after about two months trial, and died within about six months after retiring. John Frye was the second rider, and I was the third, and Gus Cliff was the fourth.

J. H. KEETLEY
When he was a Pony Express Rider

I made the longest ride without a stop, only to change horses. It was said to be 300 miles, and was done a few minutes inside of twenty-four hours. I do not vouch for the distance being correct, as I only have it from the division superintendent, A. E. Lewis, who said that the distance given was taken by his English roadometer which was attached to the front wheel of his buggy which he used to travel over his division with, and which was from St. Joe to Fort Kearney. The ride was made from Big Sandy to Ellwood, opposite St. Joe, carrying the eastgoing mail, and returning with the westbound mail to Seneca without a stop, not taking time to eat, but eating my lunch as I rode. No one else came within sixty miles of equaling this ride, and their time was much slower. The Pony Express, if I remember correctly, started at 4 o'clock p. m., April 16, 1860, with Alex Carlyle riding a nice brown mare, and the people came near taking all the hair out of the poor beast's tail for souvenirs. His ride was to Guittard's, 125 miles from St. Joe. He rode this once a week. The mail started as a weekly delivery, and then was increased to semi-weekly inside of two months. The horses, or relays, were supposed to be placed only ten miles apart, and traveled a little faster than ten miles per hour so as to allow time to change, but this could not always be done, as it was difficult then in the early settlement of the country to find places where one could get feed and shelter for man and beast, and sometimes horses had to go twenty-five to thirty miles, but in such cases there were more horses placed at such stations to do the work, and they did not go as often as the horses on the shorter runs. At the start the men rode from 100 to 125 miles, but after the semi-weekly started, they rode about 75 or 80 miles. My ride and those of the other boys out of St. Joe was 125 miles, to Guittard's, but later we only rode to Seneca, eighty miles. The first pony started from the one-story brick express office on the east side of Third Street, between Felix and Edmond streets, but the office was afterwards moved to the Patee House. At 7 o'clock a. m. we were ordered from the stables two blocks east of the Patee House by the firing of a cannon in front of the Patee House which was the signal for the ferry boat to come from Ellwood and to lie in waiting at the landing until our arrival. We rode into the office and put on the mail, which consisted of four small leather sacks six by twelve inches, fastened on to a square macheir which was put over the saddle. The sacks were locked with little brass locks much like one sees to-day on dog collars, and the sacks were sewed to the macheir, one in front and one behind each leg of the rider. When the mail was put on, and the rider mounted on his race horse, which was always used out of St. Joe to the Troy Station, nine miles from Ellwood, he bounded out of the office door and down the hill at full speed, when the cannon was fired again to let the boat know that the pony had started, and it was then that all St. Joe, great and small, were on the sidewalks to see the pony go by, and particularly so on the route that they knew the pony was sure to take. We always rode out of town with silver mounted trappings decorating both man and horse and regular uniforms with plated horn, pistol, scabbard, and belt, etc., and gay flower-worked leggings and plated jingling spurs resembling, for all the world, a fantastic circus rider. This was all changed, however, as soon as we got on to the boat. We had a room in which to change and to leave the trappings in until our return. If we returned in the night, a skiff or yawl was always ready and a man was there to row us across the river, and to put the horse in a little stable on the bank opposite St. Joseph. Each rider had a key to the stable. The next day we would go to the boat, cross the river, bring our regular horse and our trappings across to the St. Joe side. We stayed in St. Joe about three days and in Seneca about the same length of time, but this depended pretty much on the time that we received the mail from the West. The Pony Express was never started with a view to making it a paying investment. It was a put-up job to change the then Overland mail route which was running through Arizona on the southern route, changed to run by way of Denver and Salt Lake City, where Ben Holladay had a stage line running tri-weekly to Denver and weekly to Salt Lake. The object of the Pony Express was to show the authorities at Washington that by way of Denver and Salt Lake to Sacramento was the shortest route, and the job worked successfully, and Ben Holladay secured the mail contract from the Missouri River to Salt Lake, and the old southern route people took it from Salt Lake City to Sacramento. As soon as this was accomplished and the contract awarded, the pony was taken off, it having fulfilled its mission. Perhaps the war also had much to do with changing the route at that time. I hope the data I have given you will be satisfactory and of value to you. I have been asked for it many times, but have always refused. You will please excuse me for not sending my photo or allowing my people at home to furnish the old daugerrotype there that was taken when I made the ride as I am much opposed to publicity and newspaper notoriety or any other puffs, but it is impossible to always keep clear of reporters and to keep them from saying something. I will add that the letters were all wrapped in oil silk, in case the pony

A PRESSING SITUATION

had to swim, to keep the mail dry, and the regular charge was $5.00 a half ounce.

Yours truly,

J. H. KEETLEY.

The route of the riders from St. Joseph, after crossing the Missouri River, lay a little southwest until it struck the old military road forty-four miles out, at Kennekuk, then it turned a little northwesterly across the Kickapoo Indian Reservation, by the way of Grenada, Logchain, Seneca, Ash Point, Guittard's, Marysville, Hollenburg, up Little Blue Valley to Rock Creek, Big Sandy, Liberty Farm, over prairies to Thirty-two-mile Creek, across the divide, over sand hills and prairies to Platte River, and due west up that valley to Kearney. This was the trail taken by the Mormons in 1847, and afterward by the gold seekers to California in 1848–9, and by General Albert Sidney Johnston and his army of 5,000 men, who marched from Fort Leavenworth to Salt Lake City in 1857–8.

From Fort Kearney the train led westward 200 miles along the Platte to old Julesburg, then across the

J. H. KEETLEY
As he is to-day, a prosperous Salt Lake business man.

South Fork of the Platte northwesterly to Fort Laramie, then over the foothills at the base of the Rockies to South Pass, by Fort Bridger to Salt Lake. Thence by the route of the riders from the Sacramento end, as given heretofore, to the steamer at Sacramento for San Francisco.

Of the riders from the St. Joseph start, after those mentioned by J. H. Keetley in his letter to Mr. Wyeth, printed earlier in this chapter, Alex Carlyle, John Frye, Keetley himself, and Gus Cliff; the first named died of consumption shortly after the service was inaugurated. Frye joined the Union army as a member of Gen. Blunt's scouts, and was killed in Arkansas in 1863 in a hand-to-hand fight with a company of "Arkansas rangers" in which battle he killed with his own hand, before being overcome, no less than five of his antagonists. Gus Cliff died in Los Angeles, California, in 1865, of bronchitis, while serving with a government freighting outfit.

Melville Baughn was another of the riders who alternated with Carlyle, Frye, Keetley, and Cliff from St. Joseph to Seneca, but was afterward transferred to the Fort Kearney and Thirty-two-mile Creek. Once on this run his pony was stolen. Baughn followed the thief to Loup Creek, secured his pony, and rode back to Kearney where he found the mail pouch and finished his trip, a little behind schedule time. The record is that Baughn, a few years afterward, lost his life at the hands of the law, at Seneca, upon a charge of murder.

Jim Beatley, whose name "in the States" was Foote, rode from Seneca to Big Sandy, fifty miles, and doubled his route twice a week. He was a native of Richmond, Va., and was killed in a quarrel at Farrell's ranch in Southern Nebraska in 1862, by an Overland employe named Milt Motter.

Will Boulton, who rode opposite to Beatley, was living in Minnesota at last accounts. Once while Boulton was within five miles of his station, Guittard's, his pony becoming disabled, he was forced to abandon the animal and "foot it" with his pouch and accoutrements to the station, where he received another mount and completed his trip.

Don C. Rising for a time rode from Big Sandy to Fort Kearney. He was not seventeen, but it is reported that he made two runs, on special orders, when he averaged twenty miles an hour. He was from Steuben County, N. Y., and now resides at Wetmore, Neb.

"Little Yank" rode between Cottonwood Springs and Julesburg, and often covered 100 miles at a trip. He weighed not over one hundred pounds, and was twenty-five years old.

Hogan was the name of the rider from Julesburg to Mud Springs, near historical Chimney Rock, about eighty miles. He lives somewhere in Nebraska.

Theodore Rand's run was 110 miles, from Box Elder to Julesburg. He covered the entire distance always at night. He was a Pony Express rider from the time the system was inaugurated until it was withdrawn. While the schedule time was ten miles an hour, he generally averaged twelve miles an hour. When he first went on the line he rode each animal twenty-five miles, but later he was given a fresh horse every fifteen miles. Rand is now a railroad man living at Atchison, Kansas. James Moore, whose most remarkable rides and adventures are mentioned

Col. W. F. Cody
As he was in Union Pacific Building Days.

elsewhere in these chronicles, was one of the riders between St. Joseph and Salt Lake, as was W. F. Cody, who is also spoken of at length in a separate chapter.

Bill Cates was one of the riders along the Platte who had many exciting adventures with Indians.

James W. Brink was one of the early mail-carriers on the plains, and was one of the first Pony Express riders on the eastern half. He was known as "Dock" among the early stage drivers, and was with Hickok—Wild Bill—in the fight at Rock Creek Station when five of the McCandless band of outlaws were killed.

Upon the day of this writing the author talked with Charles Cliff—brother of Gus Cliff—at St. Joseph, Mo., where he is engaged in merchandizing. Charles was only seventeen when he was a Pony Express rider, and he was one of the most daring. He rode on alternate days from St. Joseph to Seneca, and generally covered his eighty miles in eight hours. Three years after the closing of the Pony Express enterprise he was freighting on the plains and one day became engaged in a battle with Indians. In this fight he received three bullets in his body and twenty-seven more in his clothes. His party, composed of the men necessary to the piloting of nine wagons, was besieged three days by a war band of 100 Sioux, which was held at bay until the arrival of a large train with men enough to put the Indians to flight.

Will D. Jenkins, now a distinguished citizen of Washington State, residing at Olympia, the capital, and who has frequently held high office in that commonwealth, was at times employed as a Pony Express rider, his home being at Big Sandy, Nebraska, in those days. Writing of the Pony Express he says:

"Although only a substitute, I shall always retain a certain degree of pride in the fact that I rode stations on the old Pony Express, and that at a time and place when it was far safer to be at home. I remember also Bob Emery's wild stage drive from 'The Narrows.' I was an eye witness of that exciting event. During my boyhood days on the plains I witnessed many exciting chases, but none that would compare with that wild drive. One Sioux warrior mounted on a fleeter pony than the other Indians would make a complete circle of the stage, and at each circle would send in a volley of arrows. But Bob succeeded in landing his passengers at the station, none of them injured."

Captain Levi Hensel has been for many years an honored citizen of Pueblo, Colorado, and is well known to this writer. He says in a letter:

"I had the contract to shoe the Overland stage and Pony Express horses that ran from Kennekuk to Big Sandy up to the time that I threw down my hammer and went into the army. I missed the best three years to make money by doing so, but don't regret that I helped to save the Union. Sometimes they ran ponies in from Fort Kearney and beyond to be shod. The animals that John Frye and Jim Beatley used to ride were the worst imps of Satan in the business. The only way that I could master them was to throw them and get a rope around each foot, stake them out, and have a man on the head and another on the body, while I trimmed the hoofs and nailed on the shoes. They would squeal and bite all the time I was working with them. It generally took half a day to shoe one of them. But travel! They seemed never to get tired. I knew John Frye to ride one of them fifty miles without change. He was about as tough as the ponies, and Jim Beatley was another off the same piece. Jim was murdered in some sort of a cowboy row up the road, and poor Johnnie Frye was killed on the Canadian River by bushwhackers. I saw him within a few minutes after he was killed. He was one of General Blunt's sharp-shooters, along with W. S. Tough, John Sinclair, and other of the pony riders who had turned soldier. We were returning from chasing Stan Watie and gang through the Indian Nation, almost to Bogy Depot, Texas. The scouts ran into a band of Indian bushwhackers at Canadian Crossing. Frye was one of the most noted of all the Pony Express riders, and had many hairbreadth escapes from Indians on the plains. He never knew what fear was, and several times made runs through hostile bands when others weakened."

The large newspapers of both New York and the Pacific Coast were ready patronizers of the Express. The issues of their papers were printed on tissue manufactured purposely for this novel way of transmitting the news. On the arrival of the pony from the West, the news brought from the Pacific and along the route of the trail was telegraphed from St. Joseph to the East the moment the animal arrived with his important budget.

To form some idea of the enthusiasm created by the inauguration of the Pony Express, the St. Joseph Free Democrat said in relation to this novel method of carrying the news across the continent:

"Take down your map and trace the footprints of our quadrupedantic animal: From St. Joseph, on the Missouri, to San Francisco, on the Golden Horn—two thousand miles— more than half the distance across our boundless continent; through Kansas, through Nebraska, by Fort Kearney, along the Platte, by Fort Laramie, past the Buttes, over the Rocky Mountains, through the narrow passes and along the steep defiles, Utah, Fort Bridger, Salt Lake City, he witches Brigham with his swift pony-ship—through the valleys, along the grassy slopes, into the snow, into sand, faster than Thor's Thialfi, away they go, rider and horse—did you see them?

"They are in California, leaping over its golden sands, treading its busy streets. The courser has unrolled to us the great American panorama, allowed us to glance at the home of one million people, and has put a girdle around the earth in forty minutes. Verily the riding is like the riding of Jehu, the son of Nimshi, for he rideth furiously. Take out your watch. We are eight days from New York, eighteen from London. The race is to the swift."

The expenses of the Pony Express during the part of two years that it was operated were, approximately, as follows:

Equipping the line	$100,000
Maintenance, $30,000 per month	480,000
Nevada Indian War	75,000
Miscellaneous	45,000
	$700,000

While it is true that the receipts did not reach as high as $1,000 per trip, in all they did not exceed $500,000, leaving a net loss of $200,000.

"A SHARP PRELIMINARY TUSSLE."

FAMOUS RIDES AND RIDERS

A FLANK MOVEMENT

OF the brave deeds, stirring incidents, and romantic adventures of the gallant riders of the West, and especially of the Pony Express riders and other employes of that unique organization, volumes have been written, and much must forever remain unwritten, as it cannot ever be known. Nearly all of the participants in the memorable enterprise have "gone over the Divide," and the bullet of Indian or border ruffian "blue penciled" many a story that would have been startling, ere the man who knew it best could turn it in. Perhaps the greatest physical achievement of all the performances of the horsemen of the West, as a matter of endurance, was the ride of F. X. Aubrey from the plaza of Santa Fe, N. M., to the public square at Independence, Mo., a distance of nearly 800 miles,

through a country inhabited by warlike Indians, a large part of which was then a sandy desert. It was about the year 1851 that Aubrey gave his wonderful test of human endurance, before which all other attempts of the kind pale into insignificance. He was a short, heavy set man, thirty-eight years of age, in the prime of manhood and strength. His business for ten years as a Santa Fe trader had made him perfectly familiar with the trail and all the stopping places. He was a perfect horseman, and although there were great riders in those days, none of them cared to dispute the palm with Aubrey. On a wager of $1,000, he undertook to ride alone from Santa Fe to Independence inside of six days. It was fifty-five years ago that he undertook the terrible feat. It was to be the supreme effort of his life, and he sent half a dozen of the swiftest horses ahead to be stationed at the different points for use in the ride. He left Santa Fe in a sweeping gallop, and that was the pace kept up during every hour of the time until he fell fainting from his foam-covered horse in the square at Independence. No man could keep up with the rider, and he would have killed every horse in the line rather than to have failed in the undertaking. It took him just five days and nineteen hours to perform the feat, and it cost the lives of several of his best horses. After being carried into a room at the old hotel at Independence, Aubrey lay for forty-eight hours in a dead stupor. He would never have recovered from the shock had it not been for his wonderful constitution. The feat was unanimously regarded by western men as the greatest exhibition of strength and endurance ever known on the plains.

The ride of Jim Moore, a noted frontiersman of the pioneer days, was another remarkable performance. Moore was a man of almost perfect physique; in fact, by military standards he was a model. He weighed 160 pounds, stood five feet ten inches, straight as an arrow, with good neck well set on his shoulders, small waist, but good loins, and had the limbs of a thoroughbred. No finer looking man physically ever rode a broncho than Jim Moore. He could run like an Indian, was as active as a panther, the best natured man in the world, but as courageous as a lion. He was one of the first Pony Express riders.

His route was from Midway Station, half way between Fort Kearney and Cottonwood Springs, to Julesburg, a distance of 140 miles. Moore rode the round-trip of 280 miles once a week. The stations were from ten to fourteen miles apart, and a fresh horse, Spanish blood, was obtained at each station. There was little delay in these changes of horses, as the rider gave the "coyote yell" half a mile away, and, day or night, the station men had the pony ready, so that the rider had only to dismount from one horse, saddle and mount the other, and with a dig of his spurs, he was on a run again. On each route there were two express riders, one going each way. As easy as it may seem to some for a man to bestride horse after horse for 140 miles, there were few men able to endure it. Upon the occasion of which I speak, Moore's route partner had been ailing and Moore was anticipating and dreading that he might have to double the route. In this anticipation he realized that there is a time limit to endurance, and therefore he gave the "bronchos" a little more of the steel than usual and made the trip to Julesburg in eleven hours. Arriving at Julesburg, he had his fears confirmed. His partner was in bed. He had hoped that he might have a few hours for rest, but before he had time to dismount and stretch his cramped and tired muscles, the "coyote yell" of the east-going rider was heard. He drank some cold coffee, filled his pocket with cold meat, and was in the saddle again for another 140-mile ride. In order to be able to live the route out, he sent his ponies for all there was in them, with the result that he arrived at Midway after having ridden 280 miles in twenty-two hours from the time he had left there. Ben Holladay gave him a gold watch and a certificate of this remarkable performance. Many of the old frontiersmen now living knew Moore, knew of his 280-

mile ride in twenty-two hours, and have seen the watch and certificate.

J. G. Kelley, one of the veteran riders, now living in Denver, tells his story of those eventful days, when he rode over the lonely trail carrying despatches for Russell, Majors and Waddell.

"Yes," he said, "I was a Pony Express rider in 1860, and went out with Bolivar Roberts, and I tell you to protect us from the Indians. As there were no rocks or logs in that vicinity, it was built of adobes, made from the mud on the shores of the lake. To mix this and get it to the proper consistency to mould into adobes, we tramped all day in our bare feet. This we did for a week or more, and the mud being strongly impregnated with alkali carbonate of soda, you can imagine the condition

it was no picnic. No amount of money could tempt me to repeat my experience of those days. To begin with, we had to build willow roads, corduroy fashion, across many places along the Carson River, carrying bundles of willows two and three hundred yards in our arms, while the mosquitoes were so thick that it was difficult to tell whether the man was white or black, so thickly were they piled on his neck, face, and arms.

"Arriving at the Sink of the Carson River, we began the erection of a fort of our feet. They were much swollen and resembled hams. We next built a fort at Sand Springs, twenty miles from Carson Lake, and another at Cold Springs, thirty-seven miles east of Sand Springs. At the latter station I was assigned to duty as assistant station-keeper, under Jim Mc-Naughton.

"The war against the Pi-Ute Indians was then at its height, and as we were in the middle of their country, it became necessary for us to keep a standing guard night and day. The

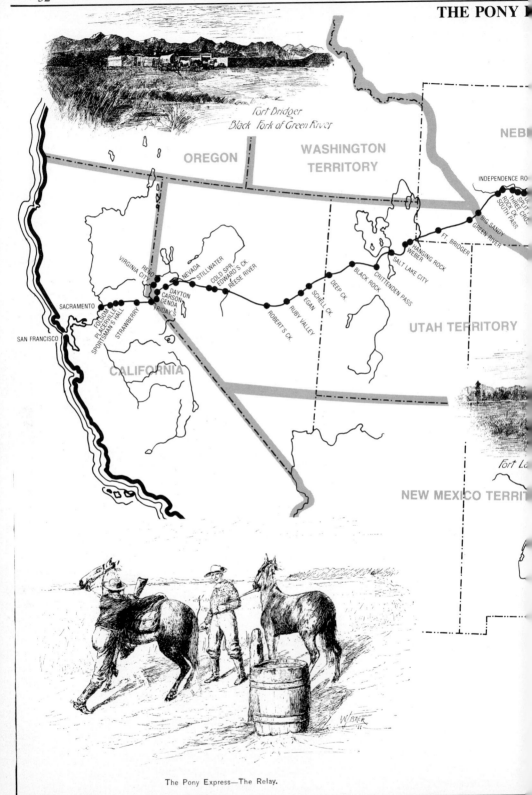

The Pony Express—The Relay.

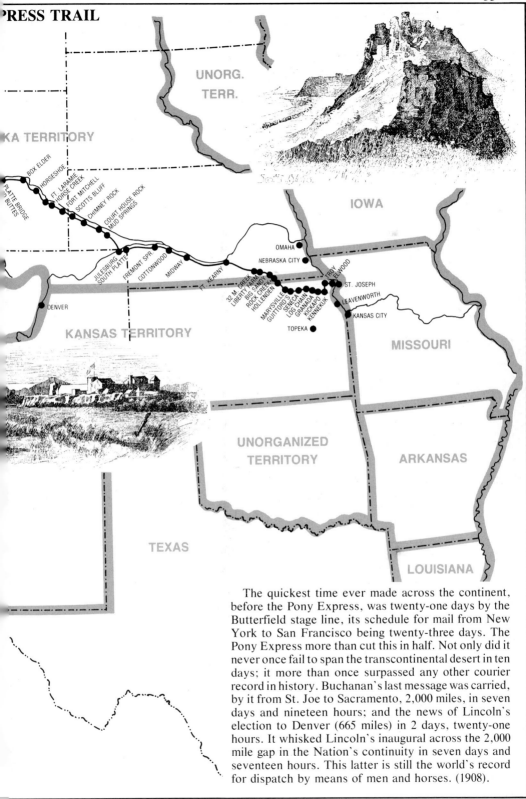

UNORG. TERR.

KA TERRITORY

IOWA

PLATTE BRIDGE
N BUTTES
BOX ELDER
HORSESHOE
FT. LARAMIE
HORSE CREEK
FORT MITCHELL
SCOTTS BLUFF
CHIMNEY ROCK
COURT HOUSE ROCK
MUD SPRINGS

JULESBURG
SOUTH PLATTE
FREMONT SPR.
COTTONWOOD
MIDWAY
FT. KEARNY

OMAHA
NEBRASKA CITY

TROY
ELWOOD
ST. JOSEPH
LEAVENWORTH

32 M. CREEK
LIBERTY FARM
BIG SANDY
ROCK CREEK
HOLLENDEN
MARYSVILLE
GUITTORD'S
SENECA
LOG CHAIN
GRANADA
KICKAPO
KENNEKUK

DENVER

KANSAS TERRITORY

TOPEKA

KANSAS CITY

MISSOURI

UNORGANIZED TERRITORY

ARKANSAS

TEXAS

LOUISIANA

The quickest time ever made across the continent, before the Pony Express, was twenty-one days by the Butterfield stage line, its schedule for mail from New York to San Francisco being twenty-three days. The Pony Express more than cut this in half. Not only did it never once fail to span the transcontinental desert in ten days; it more than once surpassed any other courier record in history. Buchanan's last message was carried, by it from St. Joe to Sacramento, 2,000 miles, in seven days and nineteen hours; and the news of Lincoln's election to Denver (665 miles) in 2 days, twenty-one hours. It whisked Lincoln's inaugural across the 2,000 mile gap in the Nation's continuity in seven days and seventeen hours. This latter is still the world's record for dispatch by means of men and horses. (1908).

Indians were often skulking around, but none of them ever came near enough for us to get a shot at him, till one dark night when I was on guard, I noticed one of our horses prick up his ears and stare. I looked in the direction indicated and saw an Indian's head projecting above the wall. My instructions were to shoot if I saw an Indian within rifle range, as that would wake the boys quicker than anything else; so I fired and missed my man.

"Later on we saw the Indian campfires on the mountain and in the morning many tracks. They evidently intended to stampede our horses, and if necessary kill us. The next day one of our riders, a Mexican, rode into camp with a bullet hole through him from the left to the right side, having been shot by Indians while coming down Edwards Creek, in the Quaking Aspen Bottom. He was tenderly cared for, but died before surgical aid could reach him.

"As I was the lightest man at the station, I was ordered to take the Mexican's place on the route. My weight was then one hundred pounds, while I now weigh one hundred and thirty. Two days after taking the route, on my return trip, I had to ride through the forest of quaking aspen where the Mexican had been shot. A trail had been cut through these little trees, just wide enough to allow horse and rider to pass. As the road was crooked and the branches came together from either side, just above my head when mounted, it was impossible for me to see ahead for more than ten or fifteen yards, and it was two miles through the forest. I expected to have trouble, and prepared for it by dropping my bridle-reins on the neck of the horse, putting my Sharp's rifle at full cock, and keeping both my spurs into the pony's flanks, and he went through that forest 'like a streak of greased lightning.'

"At the top of the hill I dismounted to rest my horse, and looking back saw the bushes moving in several places. As there were no cattle or game in that vicinity, I knew the movements to be caused by Indians, and was more positive of it, when, after firing several shots at the spot where I saw the bushes in motion, all agitation ceased. Several days after that two United States soldiers, who were on their way to their command, were shot and killed from the ambush of those bushes, and stripped of their clothing by the red devils.

"One of my rides was the longest on the route. I refer to the road between Cold Springs and Sand Springs, thirty-seven miles, and not a drop of water. It was on this ride that I made a trip which possibly gave to our company the contract for carrying the mail by stage coach across the Plains, a contract that was largely subsidized by Congress.

"One day I trotted into Sand Springs covered with dust and perspiration. Before I reached the station, I saw a number of men running toward me, all carrying rifles, and one of them with a wave of his hand said, 'All right, you pooty good boy; you go.' I did not need a second order, and as quickly as possible rode out of their presence, looking back, however, as long as they were in sight, and keeping my rifle handy.

"As I look back on those times I often wonder that we were not all killed. A short time before, Major Ormsby of Carson City, in command of seventy-five or eighty men, went to Pyramid Lake to give battle to the Pi-Utes, who had been killing emigrants and prospectors by the whole-sale. Nearly all of the command were killed. Another regiment of about seven hundred men, under the command of Colonel Daniel E. Hungerford and Jack Hayes, the noted Texas ranger, was raised. Hungerford was the beau-ideal of a soldier, as he was already the hero of three wars, and one of the best tacticians of his time. This command drove the Indians pell-mell for three miles to Mud Lake, killing and wounding them at every jump. Colonel Hungerford and Jack Hayes received, and were entitled to, great praise, for at the close of the war terms were made which have kept the Indians peaceable ever since. Jack Hayes died several years ago in Alameda, California. Colonel Hungerford, at the ripe age of seventy years, is hale and hearty, enjoying life and resting on his laurels in Italy, where he resides with his grand-daughter, the Princess Colonna.

"As previously stated, it is marvelous that the pony boys were not all killed. There were only four men at each station, and the Indians, who were then hostile, roamed over the country in bands of from thirty to a hundred.

"What I consider my most narrow escape from death was being shot at by a lot of fool emigrants, who, when I took them to task about it on my return trip, excused themselves by saying 'We thought you was an Indian.' "

Stories of the pony express riders, their adventures with Indians and outlaws, and "hairbreadth 'scapes by field and flood" could be told at sufficient length to fill a hundred volumes as large as this, but many of them were so much alike that they would appear in the narration to be

DRAWN BY FERNAND LUNGREN.

WIPING OUT A STATION.

simply repetition, yet one required as much dash and nerve as another. The service created the greatest enthusiasm, not only among the riders, but among all others of the employes and all along the route, and to aid a "pony" in trouble was jumped at as a high privilege. For instance, on the first trip the west-bound rider, between Folsom's and Sacramento, was thrown and his leg broken. A stage of the Wells-Fargo Company found him in this plight, and the special agent of the stage company volunteered to finish the ride, which he succeeded in doing so well as to arrive at Sacramento only one hour and thirty minutes late. This agent was J. G. McCall who was for many years afterward the Pacific Coast agent of the Erie Railroad. McCall often afterward told of the great reception that he got at Sacramento, and how the whole town turned out to enthusiastically welcome him.

The service also created much interest among Eastern newspapers, the more prominent of which kept representatives at St. Joe to collect news from this source. Henry Villard, afterward president of the Northern Pacific, was at the time under consideration the representative of the New York Tribune.

Beside "Buffalo Bill" and "Pony Bob," written of at length later in these chronicles, those of the pony riders who have been heard of within the last few years are these:

Jay G. Kelley was captain of Co. C., First Nevada Infantry, during the Civil War, after which he resumed the business of mining and was engaged at that at last accounts. Sam and Jim Gilson long ago became millionaires at mining in Utah. Mike Kelley became a successful miner at Austin, Nevada. Jim Bucklin, "Black Sam," Jim and Bill McNaughton died many years ago. Bill Carr was hanged at Carson,

Nevada, for the murder of Bernard Cherry, his being the first legal execution in that territory. H. J. Faust became a prominent physician in Utah. Of "Irish Tom" and Jose Zongoltz, nothing has been learned since the service ended.

Among other noted Pony Express riders, not specially mentioned elsewhere in these pages, were Jim Clark, George Spurr, Henry Wallace, George Towne, Jim McDonald, Wm. James, John Burnett, Jim Bucklin, Wm. Carr, Wm. Carrigan, Major Egan, J. K. Ellis, H. J. Faust, John Fisher Jim Gentry, Jim Gilson, Sam Gilson, Lee Huntington, James William, Bob Martin, J. G. McCall, Jim McNaughton, Josh Perkins, Johnson Richardson, Bart Riles, George Thacher, Henry Wallace, Dan Wescott, and as many more whose names and gallant deeds are lost from the records as have been the names and deeds of thousands of other heroes who helped to make the great West the rich heritage of pioneer valor, endurance, and enterprise.

Among the humorous incidents associated with the Pony Express was one associated with "Artemus Ward" — Charles Farrar Browne — that has come to be a joke classic.

ARTEMUS WARD

Artemus was at the zenith of his fame as a humorous writer and lecturer at the time of the starting of the Pony Express. Thomas Maguire, the most prominent promoter of amusements in San Francisco at that time, desired to employ Ward for a series of entertainments in California. He sent one of the expensive dispatches from San Francisco to New York asking Ward:

"What will you take for a hundred nights?"

Ward promptly responded, by the same means:

"Brandy and water."

Artemus made the trip to California, going by steamer via Panama, and returning overland. The engagement was profitable and hilarious to Artemus and Maguire, and gave much joy to the genial humorist's audiences everywhere, en route.

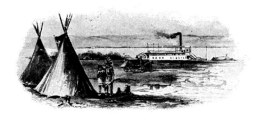

DRAWN BY FERNAND LUNGREN.

THE COOK.

"PONY BOB" — ROBERT HASLAM

"Pony Bob"—from a painting by H. H. Cross
The rider is pictured as carrying the news of Lincoln's election as President, riding 120 miles, in 8 hours, 10 minutes using 13 relays of horses. He was ambushed by Indians, shot with flint-head arrows through the lower jaw, fracturing it on both sides and knocking out 5 teeth.

AS nervy and daring as possible for a man to be, and the most famous of the Pony Express riders, except Col. W. F. Cody, "Buffalo Bill," was Robert Haslam, known throughout the West as "Pony Bob," and yet so-called by his intimates. He was the hero of many fights with Indians and "road agents," and the principal actor in such a number of hair-breadth escapes and all manner of peril incident to the westward trail that they alone would make a great volume of intense and strenuous adventure.

In his own modest way Mr. Haslam tells here of some of these and others are briefly told by persons acquainted with the facts as participants in the history-making of those times.

"About eight months after the Pony Express was established, the Pi-Ute War commenced in Nevada," says Mr. Haslam. "Virginia City, then the principal point of interest, and hourly expecting an attack from the hostile Indians, was only in its infancy. A stone hotel on C Street was in course of construction and had reached an elevation of two stories. This was hastily transformed into a fort for the protection of the women and children. From the city the signal fires of the Indians could be seen on every mountain peak, and all available men and horses were pressed into service to repel the impending assault of the savages.

"When I reached Reed's Station,

marshal for Utah, and Haslam was appointed deputy marshal, but that business not being to his liking, he became again an employe of the Wells-Fargo Company, as first messenger from Salt Lake City to Denver, 720 miles by stage, and filled that position for several years.

At this writing, the autumn of 1907, Mr. Haslam, who is still called "Pony Bob" by his intimates, is a hale, happy, and prosperous citizen of Chicago, attending industriously every day to his business, which is associated with the management of the vast Congress Hotel organization that includes the Auditorium Hotel and its magnificent annexes.

To see Mr. Haslam as he is in the conventional garb and quiet calling that are now of his life, one would find a test of credulity when informed that the bland, mild mannered, and affable gentleman indicated had ever experienced the dangers, privations, and hazardous adventures that have marked the career of "Pony Bob" in blazing the western way.

PONY BOB AS HE IS TO-DAY

COL. W. F. CODY
"BUFFALO BILL"

"BUFFALO BILL" — COL. W. F. CODY

ON "Cody Day" at the Trans-Mississippi Exposition in Omaha, in the summer of 1898, this writer had the good fortune to be among the guests at a banquet given by distinguished citizens to Col. W. F. Cody, famed throughout the world as "Buffalo Bill." On this occasion Col. Alexander Majors, frequently mentioned in these chronicles, told in a speech at the table of how Will Cody, a fatherless western lad, whose sire had been slain by Indians, came to him for employment, and how he had engaged the boy to ride as a messenger between the freight trains of great wagons that the firm of Russell, Majors and Waddell were at that time sending to and fro in long caravans across the western plains.

Col. Majors spoke in high laudation and deep affection of Cody, both as man and boy, and told much concerning this famous plainsman's career as messenger, Pony Express rider, guide, hunter, and Indian fighter. Among other things he told of how Will Cody, when he received his first month's pay, which was a considerable sum for a boy in his "teens" to earn, took the coin to his mother, and in his exhilaration spread it out over the table and said: "Ain't it splendid, mother, that I can get all this money for you and my sisters?"

Some one in the party exclaimed, much to the amusement of the banqueters: "Yes, and he has been spreading it ever since."

Col. Majors dwelt with the eloquence of truth, high character, earnestness, and affection upon the faithfulness and intrepidity of Cody, and mentioned that part of the line over which Cody rode in the express service as being particularly hazardous. This route lay between Red Buttes and Three Crossings, so called because the trail ran through a cañon where the Sweetwater reached from wall to wall, and had to be crossed three times in a short distance. It was a most dangerous, long, and lonely trail, including the perilous crossing of the North Platte River, which at that place was half a mile wide, and, though generally shallow, in some places reached a depth of twelve feet, a stream often much swollen and very turbulent. An average of fifteen miles an hour had to be made, including change of horses, detours for safety, and time for meals.

He passed through many a gauntlet of death in his flight from station to station, bearing express matter that was of the greatest value.

Colonel Cody, in telling the story of his own experiences with the Pony Express, says:

"The enterprise was just being started. The line was stocked with horses and put into good running order. At Julesburg I met Mr. George Chrisman, the leading wagon-master of Russell, Majors and Waddell, who had always been a good friend to me. He had bought out 'Old Jules,' and was then the owner of Julesburg Ranch, and the agent of the Pony Express line. He hired me at once as a Pony Express rider, but as I was so young he thought I was not able to stand the fierce riding which was required of the messengers. He knew, however, that I had been raised in the saddle, that I felt more at home there than in any other

place, and as he saw that I was confident that I could stand the racket, and could ride as far and endure it as well as some of the old riders, he gave me a short route of forty-five miles, with the stations fifteen miles apart, and three changes of horses. I was fortunate in getting well-broken animals, and being so light I easily made my forty-five miles on my first trip out, and ever afterward.

"As the warm days of summer approached, I longed for the cool air of the mountains; and to the mountains I determined to go. When I returned to Leavenworth I met my old wagon-master and friend, Lewis Simpson, who was fitting out a train at Atchison and loading it with supplies for the Overland Stage Company, of which Mr. Russell, my old employer, was one of the proprietors. Simpson was going with this train to Fort Laramie and points farther west.

" 'Come along with me, Billy,' said he. 'I'll give you a good lay-out. I want you with me.'

" 'I don't know that I would like to go as far west as that again,' I replied. 'But I do want to ride the Pony Express once more; there's some life in that.'

" 'Yes, that's so; but it will soon shake the life out of you,' said he. 'However, if that's what you've got your mind set on, you had better come to Atchison with me and see Mr. Russell, who, I'm pretty certain, will give you a situation.'

"I met Mr. Russell there and asked him for employment as a Pony Express rider; he gave me a letter to Mr. Slade, who was then the stage-agent for the division extending from Julesburg to Rocky Ridge. Slade had his headquarters at Horseshoe Station, thirty-six miles west of Fort Laramie, and I made the trip thither

in company with Simpson and his train

"Almost the first person I saw after dismounting from my horse was Slade. I walked up to him and presented Mr. Russell's letter, which he hastily opened and read. With a sweeping glance of his eye he took my measure from head to foot, and then said:

" 'My boy, you are too young for a Pony Express rider. It takes men for that business.'

" 'I rode two months last year on Bill Trotter's division, sir, and filled the bill then; and I think I am better able to ride now,' said I.

" 'What! Are you the boy that was riding there, and was called the youngest rider on the road?'

" 'I am the same boy,' I replied, confident that everything was now all right for me.

" 'I have heard of you before. You are a year or so older now, and I think you can stand it. I'll give you a trial, anyhow, and if you weaken you can come back to Horseshoe Station and tend stock.' "

"Thus ended our interview. The next day he assigned me to duty on the road from Red Buttes on the North Platte to the Three Crossings of the Sweetwater—a distance of seventy-six miles—and I began riding at once. It was a long piece of road, but I was equal to the undertaking, and soon afterward had an opportunity to exhibit my power of endurance as a Pony Express rider.

"For some time matters progressed very smoothly, though I had no idea that things would always continue so. I was well aware that the portion of the trail to which I had been assigned was not only the most desolate and lonely, but it was more eagerly watched by the savages than elsewhere on the long route.

"Slade, the boss, whenever I arrived safely at the station, and before I started out again, was always very earnest in his suggestions to look out for my scalp.

" 'You know, Billy,' he would say, 'I am satisfied yours will not always be the peaceful route it has been with you so far. Every time you come in I expect to hear that you have met with some startling adventure that does not always fall to the average express rider.'

"I replied that I was always cautious, made detours whenever I noticed anything suspicious. 'You bet I look out for number one.' The change soon came.

"One day, when I galloped into Three Crossings, my home station, I found that the rider who was expected to take the trip out on my arrival, had gotten into a drunken row the night before and had been killed. This left that division without a rider. As it was very difficult to engage men for the service in that uninhabited region, the superintendent requested me to make the trip until another rider could be secured. The distance to the next station, Rocky Ridge, was eighty-five miles and through a very bad and dangerous country, but the emergency was great and I concluded to try it. I, therefore started promptly from Three Crossings without more than a moment's rest: I pushed on with the usual rapidity, entering every relay station on time, and accomplished the round trip of 322 miles back to Red Buttes without a single mishap and on time. This stands on

Cody on Buckskin Joe.

the records as being the longest Pony Express journey ever made.

"A week after making this trip, and

A ROW IN A CATTLE TOWN.

while passing over the route again, I was jumped on by a band of Sioux Indians who dashed out from a sand ravine nine miles west of Horse Creek. They were armed with pistols, and gave me a close call with several bullets, but it fortunately happened that I was mounted on the fleetest horse belonging to the express company and one that was possessed of remarkable endurance. Being cut off from retreat back to Horseshoe, I put spurs to my horse, and lying flat on his back, kept straight for Sweetwater, the next station, which I reached without accident, having distanced my pursuers. Upon reaching that place, however, I found a sorry condition of affairs, as the Indians had made a raid on the station the morning of my adventure with them, and after killing

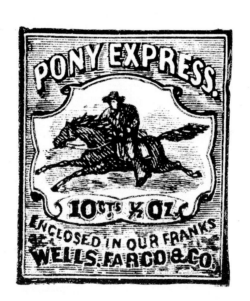

the stock tender had driven off all the horses, so that I was unable to get a remount. I, therefore, continued on to Ploutz' Station, twelve miles farther, thus making twenty-four miles straight run with one horse. I told the people at Ploutz what had happened at Sweetwater Bridge, and went on and finished the trip without any further adventure.

"About the middle of September, the Indians became very troublesome on the line of the stage road along the Sweetwater. Between Split Rock and Three Crossings they robbed a stage, killed the driver and two passengers, and badly wounded Lieutenant Flowers, the assistant division agent. The red-skinned thieves also drove off the stock from the different stations, and were continually lying in wait for the passing stages and Pony Express riders, so that we had to take many desperate chances in running the gauntlet.

"The Indians had now become so bad and had stolen so much stock that it was decided to stop the Pony Express for at least six weeks, and to run the stages only occasionally during that period; in fact, it would have been impossible to continue the enterprise much longer without restocking the line.

"While we were thus all lying idle, a party was organized to go out and search for stolen stock. This party was composed of stage drivers, express riders, stock tenders, and ranchmen—forty of them altogether—and they were well armed and well mounted. They were mostly men who had undergone all kinds of hardships and braved every danger, and they were ready and anxious to 'tackle' any number of Indians. Wild Bill, who had been driving stage on the road and had recently come down to our division, was elected captain of the company. It was supposed that the stolen stock had been taken to the head of the Powder River and vicinity, and the party, of which I was a member, started out for that section in high hopes of success.

"Twenty miles out from Sweetwater Bridge, at the head of Horse Creek, we found an Indian trail running north toward Powder River, and we could see by the tracks that most of the horses had been recently shod and were undoubtedly our stolen stage stock. Pushing rapidly forward, we followed this trail to Powder River; thence down this stream to within about forty miles of the spot where old Fort Reno now stands. Here the trail took a more westerly course along the foot of the mountains, leading eventually to Crazy Woman's Fork—a tributary of Powder River. At this point we discovered that the party whom we were trailing had been joined by another band of Indians, and judging from the fresh appearance of the trail, the united body could not have left this spot more than twenty-four hours before.

"Being aware that we were now in the heart of the hostile country and might at any moment find more Indians than we had lost, we advanced with more caution than usual and kept a sharp lookout. As we were approaching Clear Creek, another tributary of Powder River, we discovered Indians on the opposite side of the creek, some three miles distant; at least we saw horses grazing, which was a sure sign that there were Indians there.

"The Indians, thinking themselves in comparative safety, never before having been followed so far into their own country by white men, had neg-

lected to put out any scouts. They had no idea that there were any white men in that part of the country. We got the lay of their camp, and then held a council to consider and mature a plan for capturing it. We knew full well that the Indians would outnumber us at least three to one, and perhaps more. Upon the advice and suggestion of Wild Bill, it was finally decided that we should wait until it was nearly dark, and then after creeping as close to them as possible, make a dash through their camp, open a general fire on them, and then stampede the horses.

"This plan, at the proper time, was very successfully executed. The dash upon the enemy was a complete surprise to them. They were so overcome with astonishment that they did not know what to make of it. We could not have astounded them any more had we dropped down into their camp from the clouds. They did not recover from the surprise of this sudden charge until after we had ridden pell-mell through their camp and got away with our own horses as well as theirs. We at once circled the

JAMES B. HICKOK
Known as "Wild Bill." In one fight, single-handed and alone, he killed ten desperadoes

SITTING BULL
Chief of Dakota Sioux-Uncapapas

horses around toward the south, and after getting them on the south side of Clear Creek, some twenty of our men, just as the darkness was coming on, rode back and gave the Indians a few parting shots. We then took up our line of march for Sweetwater Bridge, where we arrived four days afterward with all our own horses and about one hundred captured Indian ponies.

"The expedition had proved a grand success, and the event was celebrated in the usual manner—by a grand spree. The only store at Sweetwater Bridge did a rushing business for several days. The returned stock hunters drank and gambled and fought. The Indian ponies, which had been distributed among the captors, passed from hand to hand at almost every deal of cards. There seemed to be no limit to the rioting and carousing; revelry reigned supreme. On the third day of the orgy, Slade, who had heard the news, came up to the bridge and took a hand in the 'fun,' as it was called. To add some variation and excitement to the occasion, Slade got into a quarrel with a stage driver and shot him, killing him almost instantly.

"The boys became so elated as well as 'elevated' over their success against the Indians, that most of them were in favor of going back and cleaning out the whole Indian race. One old driver especially, Dan Smith, was eager to open a war on all the hostile nations, and had the drinking been continued another week he certainly would have undertaken the job, single handed and alone. The spree finally came to an end; the men sobered down and abandoned the idea of again invading the hostile country. The recovered horses were replaced on the road, and the stages and Pony Express again began running on time.

"Slade, having taken a great fancy to me, said, 'Billy, I want you to come down to my headquarters, and I'll make you a sort of supernumerary rider, and send you out only when it is necessary.'

"I accepted the offer and went with him down to Horseshoe, where I had a comparatively easy time of it. I had always been fond of hunting, and I now had a good opportunity to gratify my ambition in that direction, as I had plenty of spare time on my hands. In this connection I will relate one of my bear hunting adventures. One day, when I had nothing else to do, I saddled up an extra Pony Express horse, struck out for the foot-hills of Laramie Peak for a bear hunt. Riding carelessly along, and breathing the cool and bracing mountain air which came down from the slopes, I felt as only a man can feel who is roaming over the prairies of the far West, well armed and mounted on a fleet and gallant steed. The perfect freedom which he enjoys is in itself a refreshing stimulant to the mind as well as the body. Such indeed were my feelings on this beautiful day as I rode up the valley of the Horseshoe. Occasionally I scared up a flock of sage hens or a jack rabbit. Antelopes and deer were almost always in sight in any direction, but, as they were not the kind of game I was after on that day, I passed them by and kept on toward the mountains. The farther I rode the rougher and wilder became the country, and I knew that I was approaching the haunts of the bear. I did not discover any, however, although I saw plenty of tracks in the snow.

"About two o'clock in the afternoon, my horse having become tired, and myself being rather weary, I shot a sage hen, and, dismounting, I unsaddled my horse and tied him to a small tree, where he could easily feed on the mountain grass. I then built a little fire, and broiling the chicken and seasoning it, with salt and pepper which I had obtained from my saddlebags, I soon sat down to a 'genuine square meal,' which I greatly relished.

"After resting for a couple of hours, I remounted and resumed my upward trip to the mountain, having made up my mind to camp out that night rather than go back without a bear, which my friends knew I had gone out for. As the days were growing short, night soon came on, and I looked around for a suitable camping place. While thus engaged, I scared up a flock of sage hens, two of which I shot, intending to have one for supper and the other for breakfast.

"By this time it was becoming quite dark, and I rode down to one of the little mountain streams, where I found an open place in the timber suitable for a camp. I dismounted, and after unsaddling my horse and hitching him to a tree, I prepared to start a fire. Just then I was startled by hearing a horse whinnying farther up the stream. It was quite a surprise to me, and I immediately ran to my animal to keep him from answering as horses usually do in such cases. I thought that the strange horse might belong to some roaming band of Indians, as I knew of no white men being in that portion of the country at that time. I was certain that the owner of the strange horse could not be far distant, and I was very anxious to find out who my neighbor was, before letting him know that I was in his vicinity. I, therefore, resaddled my horse, and leaving him tied so that I could easily reach him, I took my gun and started out on a scouting expedition up the stream. I had gone about four hundred yards when, in a bend of the stream, I discovered ten or fifteen horses grazing. On the opposite side of the creek a light was shining high up the mountain bank. Approaching the mysterious spot as cautiously as possible, and when within a few yards of the light, which I discovered came from a dugout in the mountain side, I heard voices, and soon I was able to distinguish the words, as they proved to be in my own language. Then I knew that the occupants of the dugout were white men. Thinking that they might be a party of trappers, I boldly walked up to the door and knocked for admission. The voices instantly ceased, and for a moment a deathlike silence reigned inside. Then there seemed to follow a kind of hurried whispering—a sort of consultation—and then some one called out:

" 'Who's there?'

THE OUTLYING CAMP.

"'A friend and a white man,' I replied.

"The door opened, and a big ugly-looking fellow stepped forth and said:

"'Come in.'

"I accepted the invitation with some degree of fear and hesitation, which I endeavored to conceal, as I thought it was too late to back out, and that it would never do to weaken at that point, whether they were friends or foes. Upon entering the dugout my eyes fell upon eight as rough and villianous looking men as I ever saw in my life. Two of them I instantly recognized as teamsters who had been driving in Lew Simpson's train, a few months before, and had been discharged.

"They were charged with the murdering and robbing of a ranchman; and, having stolen his horses, it was supposed that they had left the coun-try. I gave them no signs of recognition, however, deeming it advisable to let them remain in ignorance as to who I was. It was a hard crowd, and I concluded the sooner I could get away from them the better it would be for me. I felt confident that they were a band of horse thieves.

"'Where are you going, young man, and who's with you?' asked one of the men, who appeared to be the leader of the gang.

"'I am entirely alone. I left Horseshoe Station this morning for a bear hunt, and not finding any bears I had determined to camp out for the night and wait till morning,' said I; 'and just as I was going into camp a few hundred yards down the creek, I heard one of your horses whinnying, and then I came to your camp.'

"I thus was explicit in my statement, in order, if possible, to satisfy the cut-throats that I was not spying upon them, but that my intrusion was entirely accidental.

"'Where's your horse?' demanded the boss thief.

"'I left him down at the creek,' I answered.

"They proposed going after the horse, but I thought that would never do, as it would leave me without any means of escape, and I accordingly said, in hopes to throw them off the track, 'Captain, I'll leave my gun here and go down and get my horse, and come back and stay all night.'

"I said this in as cheerful and as careless a manner as possible, so as not to arouse their suspicions in any way or lead them to think that I was aware of their true character. I hated to part with my gun, but my suggestion of leaving it was a part of the plan of escape which I had arranged. If they have the gun, thought I, they will surely believe that I intend to come back. But this little game did not work at all, as one of the desperadoes spoke up and said:

"'Jim and I will go down with you after your horse, and you can leave your gun here all the same, as you'll not need it.'

"'All right,' I replied, for I could certainly have done nothing else. It became evident to me that it would be better to trust myself with two men than with the whole party. It was apparent from this time on I would have to be on the alert for some good opportunity to give them the slip.

"'Come along,' said one of them, and together we went down the creek, and soon came to the spot where my horse was tied. One of the men unhitched the animal, and said, 'I'll lead the horse.'

"'Very well,' said I; 'I've got a couple of sage hens here. Lead on.'

"I picked up the sage hens which I had killed a few hours before, and followed the man who was leading the horse, while his companion brought up the rear. The nearer we approached the dugout, the more I dreaded the idea of going back among the villainous cut-throats. My first plan of escape having failed, I now determined upon another. I had both of my revolvers with me, the thieves not having thought it necessary to search me. It was now quite dark, and I purposely dropped one of the sage hens, and asked the man behind me to pick it up. While he was hunting for it on the ground, I quickly pulled out one of my Colt's revolvers and struck him a tremendous blow on the back of the head, knocking him senseless to the ground. I then instantly wheeled around and saw that the man ahead, who was only a few feet distant, had heard the blow and had turned to see what was the matter, his hand upon his revolver We faced each other at about the same instant, but before he could fire, as he tried to do, I shot him dead in his tracks. Then jumping on my horse, I rode down the creek as fast as possible, through the darkness and over the rough ground and rocks.

"The other outlaws in the dugout, having heard the shot which I had fired, knew there was trouble, and they all came rushing down the creek. I suppose by the time they reached the man whom I had knocked down, that he had recovered and hurriedly told them of what had happened. They did not stay with the man whom I had shot, but came on in hot pursuit of me. They were not mounted, and were making better time down the rough mountain than I was on horse-

back. From time to time I heard them gradually gaining on me.

"At last they came so near that I saw that I must abandon my horse. So I jumped to the ground, and gave him a hard slap with the butt of one of my revolvers, which started him on down the valley, while I scrambled up the mountain side. I had not ascended more than forty feet when I heard my pursuuers coming closer and closer; I quickly hid behind a large pine tree, and in a few moments they all rushed by me, being led on by the rattling footsteps of my horse, which they heard ahead of them. Soon they began firing in the direction of the horse, as they no doubt

supposed I was still seated on his back. As soon as they had passed me I climbed further up the steep mountain, and knowing that I had given them the slip, and feeling certain I could keep out of their way, I at once struck out for Horseshoe Station, which was twenty-five miles distant. I had very hard traveling at first, but upon reaching lower and better ground I made good headway, walking all night and getting into the station just before daylight—footsore, weary, and generally played out.

"I immediately waked up the men of the station and told them of my adventure. Slade himself happened to be there, and he at once organized a party to go out in pursuit of the horse thieves. Shortly after daylight twenty well armed stage drivers, stock tenders, and ranchmen were galloping in the direction of the dugout. Of course I went along with the party, notwithstanding that I was very tired and had had hardly time for any rest at all. We had a brisk ride, and arrived in the immediate vicinity of the thieves' rendezvous at about ten o'clock in the morning. We approached the dugout cautiously, but upon getting in close proximity to it we could discover no horses in sight. We could see the door of the dugout standing wide open, and we marched up to the place. No one was inside, and the general appearance of everything indicated that the place had been deserted—that the birds had flown. Such, indeed, proved to be the case.

"We found a new-made grave, where they had evidently buried the man whom I had shot. We made a thorough search of the whole vicinity, and finally found their trail going southeast in the direction of Denver. As it would have been useless to follow them, we rode back to the station, and thus ended my eventful bear-hunt. We had no trouble for some time after that."

A friend, who was once a station agent, tells two more adventures of Cody's: "It had become known in some mysterious manner, past finding out, that there was to be a large sum of money sent through by Pony Express, and that was what the road agents were after.

"After killing the other rider, and failing to get the treasure, Cody very naturally thought that they would make another effort to secure it; so when he reached the next relay station, he walked about a while longer than was his wont.

"This was to perfect a little plan he had decided upon, which was to take a second pair of saddle pouches and put something in them and leave them in sight, while those that held the valuable express packages he folded up in his saddle blanket in such a way that they could not be seen unless a search was made for them. The truth was Cody knew that he carried the valuable package, and it was his duty to protect it with his life.

"So with the clever scheme to outwit the road agents, if held up, he started once more upon his flying trip. He carried his revolver ready for instant use and flew along the trail with every nerve strung to meet any danger which might confront him. He had an idea where he would be halted, if halted at all, and it was a lonesome spot in a valley, the very place for a deed of crime.

"As he drew near the spot he was on the alert, and yet when two men suddenly stepped out from among the shrubs and confronted him, it gave him a start in spite of his nerve. They had him covered with rifles and brought him to a halt with the words: 'Hold! Hands up, Pony Express Bill, for we knew yer, my boy, and what yer carried.'

" 'I carry the express; and it's hanging for you two if you interfere with me,' was the plucky response.

" 'Ah, we don't want you, Billy, unless you force us to call in your checks; but it's what you carry we want.'

" 'It won't do you any good to get the pouch, for there isn't anything valuable in it,'

" 'We are to be the judges of that, so throw us the valuable or catch a bullet. Which shall it be, Billy?'

"The two men stood directly in front of the pony rider, each one covering him with a rifle, and to resist was certain death. So Cody began to unfasten his pouches slowly, while he said, 'Mark my words, men, you'll hang for this.'

" 'We'll take chances on that, Bill.'

"The pouches being unfastened now, Cody raised them with one hand, while he said in an angry tone, 'If you will have them, take them.' With this he hurled the pouches at the head of one of them, who quickly dodged and turned to pick them up, just as Cody fired upon the other with his revolver in his left hand.

"The bullet shattered the man's arm, while, driving the spurs into the flanks of his mare, Cody rode directly over the man who was stooping to pick up the pouches, his back turned to the pony rider.

"The horse struck him a hard blow that knocked him down, while he half fell on top of him, but was recovered by a touch of the spurs and bounded on, while the daring pony rider gave a wild triumphant yell as he sped on like the wind.

"The fallen man, though hurt scrambled to his feet as soon as he could, picked up his rifle, and fired after the retreating youth, but without effect, and young Cody rode on, arriving at the station on time, and reported what had happened.

"He had, however, no time to rest, for he was compelled to start back with his express pouches. He thus made the remarkable ride of 324 miles without sleep, and stopping only to eat his meals, and resting then but a few moments. For saving the express pouches he was highly complimented by all, and years afterward he had the satisfaction of seeing his prophecy regarding the two road agents verified, for they were both captured and hanged by vigilantes for their many crimes."

" 'There's Injun signs about, so keep your eyes open.' So said the station boss of the Pony Express, addressing young Cody, who had dashed up to the cabin, his horse panting like a hound, and the rider ready for the 15-mile flight to the next relay. 'I'll be on the watch, boss, you bet,' said the pony rider, and with a yell to his fresh pony he was off like an arrow from a bow.

"Down the trail ran the fleet pony like the wind, leaving the station quickly out of sight, and dashing at once into the solitude and dangers of the vast wilderness. Mountains were upon either side, towering cliffs here and there overhung the trail, and the wind sighed through the forest of pines like the mourning of departed spirits. Gazing ahead, the piercing eyes of the young rider saw every tree, bush, and rock, for he knew but too well that a deadly foe, lurking in ambush, might send an arrow or a bullet to his heart at any moment. Gradually far down the valley, his quick glance fell upon a dark object above the bowlder directly in his trail.

"He saw the object move and disappear from sight down behind the rock. Without appearing to notice it, or checking his speed in the slightest, he held steadily upon his way. But he took in the situation at a glance, and saw that on one side was a fringe of heavy timber, upon the other a precipice, at the base of which were massive rocks.

" 'There is an Indian behind that rock, for I saw his head,' muttered the young rider, as his horse flew on. Did he intend to take his chances and dash along the trail directly by his ambushed foe? It would seem so, for he still stuck to the trail.

"A moment more and he would be within range of a bullet, when suddenly dashing his spurs into the pony's side, Billy Cody wheeled to the right, and in an oblique course headed for the cliff. This proved to the foe in ambush that he was suspected, if not known, and at once there came the crack of a rifle, the puff of smoke rising above the rock where he was concealed. At the same moment a yell went up from a score of throats, and out of the timber on the other side of the valley darted a number of Indians, and these rode to head off the rider.

"Did he turn back and seek safety in a retreat to the station? No! he was made of sterner stuff and would run the gauntlet.

"Out from behind the bowlder, where they had been lying in ambush, sprang two braves in all the glory of their war paint. Their horses were in the timber with their comrades, and, having failed to get a close shot at the pony rider, they sought to bring him down at long range with their rifles. The bullets pattered under the hoofs of the flying pony, but he was unhurt, and his rider pressed him to his full speed.

"With set teeth, flashing eyes, and determined to do or die, Will Cody rode on in the race for life, the Indians on foot running swiftly toward him, and the mounted braves sweeping down the valley at full speed.

"The shots of the dismounted Indians failing to bring down the flying pony or their human game, the mounted redskins saw that their only chance was to overtake their prey by their speed. One of the number, whose war bonnet showed that he was

a chief, rode a horse that was much faster than the others, and he drew quickly ahead. Below, the valley narrowed to a pass not a hundred yards in width, and if the pony rider could get to this wall ahead of his pursuers, he would be able to hold his own along the trail in the 10-mile run to the next relay station.

"But, though he saw that there was no more to fear from the two dismounted redskins, and that he would come out well in advance of the band on horseback, there was one who was most dangerous. That one was the chief, whose fleet horse was bringing him on at a terrible pace, and threatening to reach there at the same time with the pony rider.

"Nearer and nearer the two drew toward the path, the horse of Cody slightly ahead, and the young rider

SHORT BULL,
War Chief
KICKING BEAR,
Medicine man
Ogallala Sioux, leaders of Ghost Dance War
and Messiah Craze

knew that a death struggle was at hand. He did not check his horse, but kept his eyes alternately upon the pass and the chief. The other Indians he did not then take into consideration. At length that happened for which he had been looking.

"When the chief saw that he would come out of the race some thirty yards behind his foe, he seized his bow and quick as a flash had fitted an arrow for its deadly flight. But in that instant Cody had also acted, and a revolver had sprung from his belt and a report followed the touching of the trigger. A wild yell burst from the lips of the chief, and he clutched madly at the air, reeled, and fell from his saddle, rolling over like a ball as he struck the ground.

"The death cry of the chief was echoed by the braves coming on down the valley, and a shower of arrows was sent after the fugitive pony rider. An arrow slightly wounded his horse, but the others did no damage, and in another second Cody had dashed into the pass well ahead of his foes. It was a hot chase from then on until the pony rider came within sight of the next station, when the Indians drew off and Cody dashed in on time, and in another minute was away on his next run."

On one of Cody's rides he was halted in the cañon one day by an outlaw named————, who said to him:

"You are a mighty little feller to be takin' such chances as this."

"I'm as big as any other feller," said Cody.

"How do you make that out?" the highwayman asked.

"Well, you see Colonel Colt has done it," the youngster replied, presenting at the same time a man's size revolver of the pattern that was so prevalent and useful among the men of the frontier. "And I can shoot as hard as if I was Gin'ral Jackson," he added.

"I spect you kin an' I reckon you would," was the laconic response of the lone highwayman as with a chuckle he turned up a small cañon toward the north. Cody flew on as if he were going for the doctor. The man escaped the law, reformed, and became a respectable citizen-farmer in Kansas, and in 1871 told this writer, in St. Joseph, Missouri, of the incident as here related.

Therefore his name is omitted.

Of all the Pony Express riders Cody has become the best known. His rank as colonel belongs to him by commission. Indeed, he has been commissioned as brigadier-general. He has also been a justice of the peace in Nebraska, and was once a member of the Legislature, which entitles him to the "Hon." that is sometimes attached to his name. But he only cares to be a colonel on the principle, perhaps, of the Kentuckian who, being addressed as "General," refused the title on the ground that there is no rank in Kentucky higher than colonel. But of all his titles Cody prefers that of "Buffalo Bill," by which he is known throughout the world, and which he obtained while filling a contract on the plains in furnishing buffalo meat to feed the workmen of General Jack Casement and brother, contractors in the building of the Union Pacific Railroad.

THE OVERLAND PONY EXPRESS AND THE TELEGRAPH

THE TELEGRAPH AND THE END

M R. EDWARD CREIGHTON— of blessed memory—had, during many years of his life, been engaged in constructing telegraph lines throughout the United States. He had long

EDWARD CREIGHTON

contemplated the construction of such a line from the Missouri River to the Pacific Coast. In 1860, after many consultations with the Western Union Telegraph Company, a preliminary survey for the line was agreed upon. Notwithstanding that the trip across the plains and mountains was a trying one at best, beset as it was in dangers from attacks by Indians and highwaymen. added to the chances of storm and flood, Mr. Creighton made the journey by Overland stage coach in the winter of the year mentioned. He halted at Salt Lake City, and there enlisted the very valuable interest and support of President Brigham Young, the great head of the Mormon church.

Desirous of also engaging the association of the California Telegraph Company in the enterprise, Mr. Creighton pressed, by saddle and horse, from Salt Lake to Sacramento, across the alkali desert and the Sierra Nevada range, in mid-winter, an appalling trip for even a hardy plainsman, inured to such journeyings, which Creighton was not. But he had a stout heart and a strong intent, added to a vigorous constitution, thus he accomplished the trip and his mission, and returned to Omaha in the spring of 1861, prepared to proceed with the work of construction.

The Government granted a subsidy of $40,000 per annum which was to go to the first company that should establish a telegraph line across that part of the continent, and this stimulated a mighty rivalry between the Creighton forces and those of the California company, the first building westwardly and the second eastwardly, each endeavoring to reach Salt Lake before the other.

Eleven hundred miles was the distance that the Creighton company had to build, while the California company's line for construction was only 450 miles, the obstacles, so far as nature was concerned, being about equal, mile for mile. The Creighton forces reached Salt Lake City with the completed line on the 17th of October, the California company connecting a week later. A telegram from ocean to ocean was sent October

24th, the line having been completed within little more than half a year from the time that construction began.

Mr. Creighton's financial interest in the line was eventually more than a million dollars. His original stock was worth $100,000 at 18 cents per share. This stock was afterward increased to $300,000, which rose to 85 cents per share, and Creighton sold an interest for $850,000, retaining $200,000 worth of stock.

Edward Creighton died in 1874, of paralysis, but there are many monuments to his memory not the least of which is Creighton College in Omaha, and the kindliest remembrance of the man by all who were acquainted with him in life.

The telegraph across the continent instantly, by the flashing of its first message, obviated the necessity for the Pony Express; the unique, highly romantic, and yet intensely practical and distinctly successful enterprise became a brilliant tradition.

Aside from the immediate purpose that it served so well, accelerating communication between the East and West at a particularly critical period, it demonstrated the feasibility of telegraph and railway lines across the continent at the latitude over which its course was laid, and was, in short, the avant courier of the mighty and progress-diffusing Union and Central Pacific Railway systems that have been, and are, the immeasurable agencies for the upbuilding of the vast and resourceful empire, the glorious West that was the "Great American Desert."

"On what a slender thread oft hang the weightiest things."

Julesburg. 1865

AN INCIDENT BETWEEN STATIONS.

THE PONY EXPRESS
in retrospect

IN AN AGE when the continent can be spanned by jet planes in a few hours, the moon has been reached by man, and outer space is the new frontier — in such an age, the idea of relays of men on horseback seems quaint and antiquated. What, then, is the reason for the fascination of the Pony Express?

It is not in the stars but within ourselves that the answer lies. The Pony Express rider is symbolic of the bold imagination, the daring enterprise, and the reckless courage which is the highest expression of the American character . . .

It is not for mere sentiment that this nation cherishes its heroes, preserves its historic places, and seizes upon the birthdays of events to celebrate the past. It is from a deep instinctive recognition that noble and inspiring patriotic traditions are the bands of steel that bind us as a nation; and that when these traditions lose their force and meaning we will disintegrate, spiritually and physically.

> Merrill J. Mattes,
> "The Pony Express: across Nebraska
> from St. Joseph to Fort Laramie"

NOTICE.

BY ORDERS FROM THE EAST,

THE PONY EXPRESS

WILL be DISCONTINUED.

The Last Pony coming this way left Atchinson, **Kansas**, yesterday.

ox-25-1t **WELLS, FARGO & CO., Agents.**